BACK TO ME

A DEVOTIONAL WALK
FOR THE COLLEGE FRESHMAN WOMAN

YOLI TAMU

We look forward to receiving your comments. Please contact us at review@yolitamu.com. Thank you.

Published by
Yoli Tamu Enterprises
Marina del Rey, California
www.yolitamu.com

Bulk copies or group sales of this book are available by contacting info@yolitamu.com

FIRST EDITION PRINTED SEPTEMBER 2017
Printed in USA

Tamu, Yoli
Back to Me: A Devotional Walk for the College Freshman Woman
First Edition.

Library of Congress Control Number: 2017912439
1. Devotional 2. College 3. Women 4. Freshman 5. Confidence

Issued also as an ebook.

ISBN: 978-0-692-93511-8

PRAISE For 🌺 The **Back to Me** Devotional

"I thoroughly enjoyed reading the chapters in this book. I was even more excited to read the stories and the experiences she had to offer our freshman women as an alumni of our distinguished institution. Yoli's content is relevant and timely for young women today. I look forward to Yoli sharing this book and her stories in person with our freshman class of young ladies upon her return to her alma mater."

ANDREW BROWN
Coordinator for New Student Orientation, Howard University

"This book provides valuable insight and wisdom that can support college Freshman on the journey to womanhood. It is an enjoyable read, designed to affirm, encourage and instill confidence in young ladies from a variety of backgrounds."

DARIN EARLEY, Ed.D
Director of Family of Schools, Loyola Marymount University

"Ms. Yoli is very open and transparent about many of her experiences in college. From the first chapter, I was drawn in by her vivid description of an unforgettable experience she had that was very personal to her. I connected with her vulnerability and courage throughout the book. Every chapter told a specific story and ended with a lesson that I know I could apply to my life right now! I'm so glad she wrote this book and boldly told her story to empower young women today. I couldn't put it down. It's a must read for sure! Can't wait to share it with my girlfriends!"

ATTIYAH JENKINS
College Student

"Yoli has a powerful story to tell. As I read the first chapter, I visualized it in a movie and had to put the book down to breathe and pray. Yoli bravely tells her story with such candor and heartfelt emotion. I love how the music and the questions help young women take self introspection seriously."

TEESHALAVONE JENKINS
Entrepreneur and Mother of College Student, Attiyah Jenkins

"As a high school educator, I was excited to read this book and offer it as a resource to my graduating senior girls. After reading just a few chapters, I knew I wanted to offer it to my niece as well. Yoli takes the reader on an unexpected journey that cleverly entertains and endears the reader to her passionate stories. The stories, the music, and the questions she asks the reader at the end of each chapter engage and challenge young women to take personal inventory of themselves in a way that is supportive and very encouraging."

TAMARA MAHONEY
High School Teacher, City of Angels Independent Study School

The **Back to Me** Devotional
TABLE OF CONTENTS

INTRODUCTION
A Devotional Walk Through This Book   7

CHAPTER 1
The Aftermath   11

CHAPTER 2
Gone Away   21

CHAPTER 3
Invincible   29

CHAPTER 4
On My Way Home   39

CHAPTER 5
Anybody Out There?   47

CHAPTER 6
So Beautiful   55

CHAPTER 7
Back to Me   63

CHAPTER 8
Holding On To Us   71

CHAPTER 9
Headlights   79

CHAPTER 10
Surrender   87

ABOUT THE AUTHOR
Yoli Tamu   93

I dedicate this book to my parents, Ken and Alpha Snell,
from whom I received my wings in an unlimited sky,
and to my parents in the arts, Professor Mike Malone and Ka-Ron
Lehman, from whom I learned to spread my wings and fly.

Introduction

A DEVOTIONAL WALK THROUGH THIS BOOK

Congratulations! You completed your exams, submitted your applications, and now you are headed to college! I am excited to help you navigate through the next four years of your life. Consider this book your personal companion as you take this unforgettable journey through some of the most important years of yo ur life. By the time you finish reading this book, you will understand just how valuable your college experience can be if you take full advantage of all it has to offer.

Get ready to be entertained and inspired by my personal journey through the stressors of college life. You will discover how I was able to minimize stress due to personal trauma, and develop healthy relationships to ultimately find the inner peace I so desperately needed.

THE JOURNEY
Each chapter of this book reads like a personal diary for

myself and a dear friend. The dear friend, in this case, is you! I begin each chapter with one powerful quote, a song lyric from my album, and a Bible scripture to support the message of the chapter.

The chapters include life-changing moments that have shaped my life today. The lessons I learned are revealed and are offered to you for your consideration. I encourage you to read the chapter, answer the questions that follow, and then play the music provided for your enjoyment and contemplation. Each chapter title is also the song title listed on the music download. Allow the music to transport you to a peaceful place and offer you time to relax, digest and enjoy the message.

THE PURPOSE
It is my desire to help make your college experience an unforgettable one. This book was written with you in mind. After spending many years teaching and mentoring young women, I was constantly asked about the trials of becoming a young woman in today's society and away from home. Many of these women confided in me with their most personal concerns because they didn't feel comfortable sharing with their mothers, and they believed I could be objective and nurturing at the same time.

I also wished I could have shared some of my most private thoughts with my mother at that age, but I never felt completely comfortable either. In many cases, my teachers and coaches filled that gap for me, so I grew to understand the emotional void these young women felt. I vowed to do my part to help them close that gap for themselves.

As you read this book and begin to take your own journey,

there will be many times in your life when you will be nudged and challenged to stand up for what you believe in. In those moments, you will discover your voice over and over again. But those moments will also surprise, frighten, and enlighten you at the same time. The question you will always face:

 "WHEN YOU KNOW BETTER, WILL YOU DO BETTER?" ... OR WILL YOU BE FORCED TO TAKE THE **SAME RIDE** AGAIN?

I selected stories that served as major turning points in my life while living away from home on a college campus. My journey was impactful because of my professors, peers, and the incredible adventures that only a college campus could provide in such a short amount of time.

I hope this book serves as a daily reminder to help you conquer many of the challenges you will face during your college years. Recognize when God is in the midst and take the time to try to identify the lessons I learned in my life and observe how they can be applied to your own.

Above all else, enjoy this fun, introspective journey through my college years!

I wouldn't change this experience for the world.

With all my love,

The **Back to Me** Devotional

Chapter 1

THE AFTERMATH

"Did you hear about the rose that grew from a crack in the concrete? Proving nature's law wrong, it learned to walk without having feet. Funny, it seems to be keeping its dreams; it learned to breathe fresh air." **Tupac Shakur**

"Everything, everything's breaking down, fallin' around us in a world crashing to the ground, our love is found...when the smoke clears all that's left is me and You."
Aftermath Lyric from my 'Back to Me' Album

"Put on all of God's armor so that you will be able to stand firm against all strategies of the devil. For we are not fighting against flesh and blood enemies, but against evil rulers and authorities of the unseen world, against mighty powers in this dark world, and against evil spirits in the heavenly places." **Ephesians 6:11-12 NLT**

THE DAY MY WORLD CHANGED FOREVER

On a beautiful day in the Spring of 1993, I had just been cleared to graduate! I did it! After 4 long years of studying, training, and dedicating my life to my craft and commitment to the performing arts, I was finally ready to graduate with a Bachelor of Fine Arts in Musical Theatre

from Howard University! I dreamed about attending this school ever since I heard the incredible Dancer, Choreographer and Director, Debbie Allen graduated from there. I wanted to learn from the professors that taught her! I knew if she went there, the sky would be the limit for what I could accomplish with my life one day! Walking home to the house I shared with 2 other roommates, the sun was shining brightly and the trees seemed to greet me as I passed them by. I was on cloud nine and couldn't wait to call home to tell my parents that it was official. I thought, "Start booking your airline tickets, folks cause I'm graduating!!!"

In all of my joy and excitement about what was to come after I prepared to walk across that stage to get my diploma, all I could think about was how much I was going to miss my friends and I wanted to do my best job for my last musical performance in the historical Ira Aldridge Theatre with the cast that had become my family over the years. Those last few weeks were becoming bittersweet, but nothing prepared me for the bitter taste of life that was about to interrupt my beautiful day.

 AS I CONTINUED MY WALK HOME, I COULD SEE MY STREET WHEN ALL OF A SUDDEN A STRANGER GRABBED ME FROM BEHIND.

He told me he had a gun and he was not going to hurt me, as he poked me with it in my side. He told me to walk with him for a while because the cops were looking for him. Startled and shocked by the abrupt surprise of someone grabbing me, I told him to calm down and I could walk for a bit, but he would have to let me go. He told me to shut up and walk. I couldn't believe it. I could see my front door just a few blocks away and I wasn't sure if I was going to be able to make that celebratory call to my parents.

Moments later, he led me behind an empty house and pushed me down the basement steps. He then told me to take my pants down. I couldn't believe what was getting ready to happen. I thought to myself, "Is he gonna rape me?" I couldn't even bear the thought. I pleaded with him and told him, "The coast is clear. There are no cops. You can still get away. Why do you want me to pull my pants down?" He said as he poked me with the gun again, "I'm not gonna ask you again." I remember thinking to myself, I've come too far and my parents have worked too hard to give me the opportunity to graduate only to let someone take it away from me in an instant. As I slowly began to pull my pants down, I remember praying to God to not let me die. I told him I could not go out this way. I told Him to help me fight and if I die in the process, tell my family I love them. In that moment, I decided to fight for my life.

I began to pull my pants back up and I opened my eyes to face my attacker. But...he was gone. I can't even explain how I didn't hear him leave, but when I opened my eyes, he was gone. I was left there pulling up my pants with no sign of the person there to attack me. I knew instantly God did it. He had to have moved him away from me. Some say I experienced an out of body experience that God protected me from. I ran home and told my roommates to call the police. How could he have

been there one minute and gone the next? Unbelievable!
God intervened and I lived and I was not raped.

In the weeks that followed, the investigator found my
attacker and he was arrested. But, the violation was
made and my life would never be the same. I would never
look at the world and all of its people the same again.
My parents were so grateful to the investigator and my
friends for being there for me, but the emotional scar
would take years to heal for myself and my family. My
family included my cast I had the pleasure of working
with. But, the one person who amazed me with his
strength and comfort the most was my professor/stage
director. He usually never showed emotion. Often, I never
knew if I was doing a good job with my characters on
stage. But when he heard about my attack, he showed
his compassion. He hugged me like I'd never hugged
him before. He told me to take some time off from
rehearsals, but to come back and do the show. He did not
want my attacker to win by getting ahold of me inside.
He told me, "You love to perform. Don't let him take that
away from you. You were born to do this. Go rest and
come back to do the amazing job you meant to do. Use
this experience to make you greater."

I took a week off to be with my mother and sister, who
flew out to see me. When I retuned back to school
to perform our last show of the season, I had to sing
a song that started with the lyric, "The courage of a
dreamer...". All I thought about was how much I dreamed
to be onstage, how God saved me that day and left me
unscathed, and how happy and supportive my family
and friends were to see me perform that song and use
my own courage to make it through to the end. I began
to gain strength from them and I was reminded that

God didn't bring me this far just to leave me. A storm came in and took away my sunshine for a little while, but my sunshine returned when I remembered who I was all along.

I was forever changed that graduation year. I discovered a new strength and resilience to continue to be my best self in the midst of pain and disappointment. God had my back and I went on to sing and graduate inspite of my tragedy! I did it anyway and so can you!

THE SKY IS THE LIMIT

It is so important to dream your biggest dream and make it your life's goal to go after all the resources, people, and experiences needed to make it happen. When you dream BIG, you require so much of yourself and the people around you. You are no longer interested in just living a comfortable life. Instead you develop a desire to be challenged and stretched in ways that push you to your greatest potential. When you dream big, you are open to new and exciting opportunities that may scare you at first, but quickly expose you to people who are on the same journey seeking the same uncomfortable ride of a lifetime!

THE BITTER TASTE OF LIFE

Life will definitely be bittersweet. Get ready for it to throw you some curve balls that will interrupt the plan you thought you had for your life. Those curveballs and interruptions will cause you to doubt yourself and wonder whether the dream was ever worth pursuing in the first place. Don't fall victim to the circumstances of your life. They are all just that, circumstances. The plan you and your Creator have designed will not be stopped permanently by your circumstances unless you allow it.

Your plans may take a turn down a different path, but the ultimate goal will always be there. With the support of your Creator and the exciting people that will come into your life, you will be guided toward your ultimate goal. All you have to do is remember what your goal is and look out for people who want to help you get there. See your circumstances as experiences that are meant to help you understand who you are and what you really stand for.

I'VE COME TOO FAR TO GIVE UP NOW! HELP ME FIGHT!

I found out what I stood for when I was attacked. In the midst of my fear, I remained focused on what I wanted out of life. I knew God did not bring me this far to let a stranger take my dream away. I decided to fight back with God's help. I knew I couldn't do it alone because I was being held at gunpoint. But, I did know that a greater Source more powerful than my attacker and me could and would intervene. How God was going to help me was unclear. But, I knew that I wanted to fight to see my parents again. I wanted to fight to walk across that stage, graduate and sing again. I had a dream for my life that I was willing to fight to see realized. You have to be that committed to your dream. Take God with you and I know you'll get there. After all, God helped you create the dream and He wants you to realize it too.

EMOTIONAL SCARS

The pain of the interruption will take time to heal. But, just like a scar on your leg that heals faster with a Band-Aid and a little ointment, family, friends and your Creator will rush in to comfort and heal you too. I thoroughly appreciated the love and comfort I received from praying to God and talking to family. But I discovered I also needed the support of a professional psychologist to help me understand what had happened to me. Many people shy away from therapy. But, I believe some scars need extra attention and a psychologist can offer that additional perspective that our loved ones cannot. Don't be afraid to heal your emotional scars with the comfort of prayer, family members, and a licensed professional. You have too much life to live. So, treat yourself to a healing process that is productive and gets you back on track.

DO IT ANYWAY

During the healing process, life will continue to interrupt your path, but stay the course. The interruption, although painful, is not as powerful as it may appear. My professor told me not to let my attacker win by giving in to my pain. So, don't let your circumstance win in the midst of your pain. Think about the joy you feel when you imagine yourself achieving your goals. Think about the support you have and will continue to receive from others as you press forward. Realize you are not in this game of life by yourself. You have an army of support just waiting to embrace you. So, in the midst of your fear and doubt, do it anyway!

THE SUN ALWAYS SHINES AGAIN

A new day awaits you. New dreams and new opportunities can't wait to meet you. When the storm subsides and the rain washes away the past, the sun will return to shine again. What will be revealed this time will be the glow of the aftermath!!

EMBRACE IT NOW!

The **Back to Me** Devotional

FOOD FOR THOUGHT

Mentors
Who do you know in your life that has inspired you to be your best and keep moving toward your dreams? What did you admire about their life that encouraged you?

_____
_____
_____
_____
_____

Support System
How reliable is your support system of family and friends? Do you have someone you can call in a real time of need?

_____
_____
_____
_____
_____

Healing Process
When you are in pain, what is your healing process? What is worth fighting for in your life today?

_____
_____
_____
_____
_____

Aftermath Glow

After the healing process begins, the glow of the aftermath will be revealed. What will your glow reflect to others watching? How will your life be different after surviving your circumstance?

_____

_____

_____

_____

_____

The **Back to Me** Devotional

GONE AWAY

"Everything will CHANGE. The only question is growing up or decaying." **Nikki Giovanni**

"No longer a glass ceiling holding me. Shattered glass falls over my head ...and I'm gone away!"
Gone Away Lyric from my 'Back to Me' Album

"Trust in the Lord with all your heart; do not depend on your own understanding. Seek His will in all you do, and He will show you which path to take." **Proverbs 3:5-6 NLT**

TAKING A RISK

My freshman year of college was full of excitement and nervous energy. I finally made it to the one school I applied for, Howard University and I actually got in! I was accepted! Just being accepted felt like a prize in itself. I remember waiting anxiously in the halls of the Fine Arts Dept. to meet one of my professors for the first time. This was the meeting that would solidify my college major. I was a dance major at my performing arts high school and I sang in church. During the summer months, I also enjoyed participating in acting workshops. So, when I

applied to Howard University, I chose Acting as a major because I was told Debbie Allen and her equally amazing sister, Phylicia Rashad pursued acting majors.

When my name was called to enter the classroom to meet the professor, my heart was beating out of my chest. I was happy and scared at the same time. I wanted to be my best and present myself well in front of the professor. I entered the room and there he was, Professor M, the man I had heard so much about from other students earlier in the hallway. They told me he was firm and he was strict, but he was one of the best instructors in the dept. They also told me he had taught Debbie Allen! So, imagine my surprise when I found out I'd be able to meet Debbie Allen's professor on my first day!!

I slowly entered the room and stood in front of him and his assistant. This stalky man with a pot belly and balding head of silvery hair greeted me with a "Hello", but he remained seated with his arms crossed. He did not ask me to sit down. Instead, he asked me to perform my monologue. I took a deep breath, walked to the center of the room and quietly got into character. I began to perform my monologue and I could hear the shaking in my voice. Fortunately, my shaking voice worked for the scene because I was playing a mother who had just lost her children at the hands of her husband, who killed them by dropping them out of a window. It was a scene from the play, "For Colored Girls Who Have Considered Suicide When the Rainbow Is Not Enough". I made it through my monologue and waited for Professor M to say something... anything!! He was so quiet as he stared at me. I wanted to ask if he liked it, but I decided to be quiet and just wait. After what seemed like an eternity, he finally spoke and said, "I understand you can sing and dance too. Is that right?" I said, "Yes. I majored in dance in high school, but I really only sang in church". He said, "Let me here you sing. Do you have a song prepared?" I thought to myself, "A song prepared? I came here to act, not sing". But of course, I wouldn't dare say that out loud. Instead I said, "Uh, well, uh I can sing 'Amazing Grace'". He said, "Let's hear it." I began to sing the song and as I began to sing it, I started to forget who was in the room and that song became a saving grace for me right in that instant. My nerves began to subside and my voice no longer shook with fear. I was singing to the Lord thanking Him for His amazing grace. It had certainly carried me through. I went into that room blind, but now I could see that He was there with me carrying me through the moment. I knew I loved to sing, but I didn't think it would feel like it did in that room outside of church. When I ended the song, I smiled inside and I was happy I did it. That song gave me the courage to stand in front of such an important man and sing my heart out.

 AFTER I FINISHED SINGING, I REMEMBER OPENING MY EYES AND ASKING PROFESSOR M IF IT WAS OK. HE SAT UP IN HIS SEAT, LOOKED AT HIS ASSISTANT AND HE SAID TO ME, "WE NEED TO CHANGE YOUR MAJOR. YOU'RE A MUSICAL THEATRE MAJOR, NOT AN ACTING MAJOR".

I was shocked to hear him say those words because I

didn't consider myself a great singer. I thought my acting would take me to places that I never dreamed of. I said to him, "Do you really think I should be a musical theatre major?" He said, "Of course". "Don't you? You're an amazing singer. Your voice deserves to be heard and I want to hear more of it." I couldn't believe he thought my voice was amazing. I knew it touched people in church and I played around with singing some in high school, but coming from the person I traveled across the country to meet was a moment I'll never forget. I wasn't sure how I would measure up against all the really great powerful singers I heard earlier that day, but Professor M knew and I decided to take the risk and I changed my major to Musical Theatre. Something told me I was destined for great things and this man was gonna help me get there!

MAKE A PLAN

When I was accepted to the one school I applied for, I was speechless. By not applying to more than one school, I took my first risk at going after what I wanted. I had tunnel vision and knew Howard was the place for me. But, knowing in my gut where I wanted to attend was not enough. I had to put forth the effort to find out just what it would take to be accepted. I met with my high school counselor and talked to other college students that I knew in my neighborhood about Howard and other HBCUs before I made the leap to apply. In other words, I did my homework. I don't encourage you to apply to only one school if you're interested in other schools. By all means, apply to those that interest you. I set a goal to study for my SATs. I shared my application essay with my parents and my English teacher, discussed my college major with my counselor, and I rehearsed my monologue daily before my audition. My passion to achieve what I wanted only happened because I had a plan. Make sure you have a plan, and then make your move.

MAKE A MOVE

Fear has a funny way of showing up even after you've made a plan and you're ready to take action. How many times have you asked yourself if you were good enough to have what you want? How many times have you allowed the naysayers, the "haters", and your negative thoughts to stop you cold in your tracks before you made the move you knew felt right in your soul? If you're anything like me, I'm guessing you have doubted yourself more times than you'd care to admit. It's ok. Fear is an emotional indicator that it's time for you to make some kind of move one way or another. Either you will retreat, fall back and convince yourself that your idea is crazy and impossible to achieve or you'll jump in and give it a try no matter what happens. Jumping in and giving it a try will not only silence the "bullies" in your head, but it will propel you to another level of understanding within yourself that will cause "fear" to take notice. When you decide to move full steam ahead, your pathway can't help but open up and accommodate you. The stronger you feel about something, the sooner God will align others to assist you or He'll cause them to step aside and watch.

MEET YOUR OPPORTUNITY

You can't lose when you convince yourself and the people around you that you intend to make your goals happen. The experience alone will offer you insight into the next steps you must take to maintain your momentum. I did not expect to sing in my acting audition. I prepared myself for a college major in Acting, but God had another plan. When I listed my singing and dancing skills on my application, Professor M took notice. I found myself caught up in the momentum of the moment and I sang for him. My preparation in acting served a purpose, but my preparation in the church served one

as well. All of my experiences led me to that moment of incredible opportunity and I was ready. I didn't know that opportunity would present itself, but it did and I seized the moment and won! I won the acceptance of the professor. I conquered the fear of not feeling good enough, and I discovered I was destined for a college major in musical theatre that I never even considered.

BELIEVE IN YOURSELF

I took the risk by taking a chance on me. I recognized my silent comfort in God, the unexpected support of my new professor, and I was wiling to open myself to a new adventure that frightened me, but excited me at the same time. When you are able to replace your expectation with something even greater than you expected, you are on your way to places you can't even imagine. What was once familiar is now gone away!

TAKE THE LEAP!

FOOD FOR THOUGHT

Procrastination
When was the last time you stopped yourself because you were afraid you weren't good enough or prepared enough to have what you wanted? How did that make you feel? Is there someone in your life that encourages you to try anyway?

_____
_____
_____
_____
_____
_____
_____
_____
_____

Goals
What important goal do you have for yourself right now? What steps will you take to help you reach it?

_____
_____
_____

Name your current skills, hobbies, and interests. What do you enjoy about these things?

_____
_____
_____

Have you ever took a chance on you before? What happened? How did you feel afterwards? Would you do it again?

_____
_____
_____

The **Back to Me** Devotional

Chapter 3

INVINCIBLE

"The greater the obstacle, the more glory in overcoming it." **Moliere**

"You're invincible! Hold your head up. Let your light show. You mean so much more!" **Invincible Lyric from my 'Back to Me' Album**

"Don't have anything to do with foolish and stupid arguments, because you know they produce quarrels. And the Lord's servant must not be quarrelsome but must be kind to everyone, able to teach, not resentful." **2 Timothy 2: 23-24 NIV**

OVERCOMING THE HATERS

Riding high after an incredible audition with the one person I couldn't wait to meet left me feeling unstoppable. I knew this college journey of mine was going to be the ride of a lifetime. I accomplished my first goal by meeting Professor M, met some incredibly talented students right away, and I was ready to soak up all that HU had to offer.

My mother and I set off to get me settled into my dorm. I stayed in Crandall Hall. I believe it was a dorm primarily for freshman girls. We were met with a nice greeting from the Resident Assistant, commonly known as the RA, who escorted us to my room. My room, my "home away from

home" was clean with a nice desk and a decent mattress on a twin bed. The closet space was minimal, but I was happy to be on my own for the first time. I could tell my mother was nervous, but I knew I would one day leave with great memories from this place.

Shortly after my mom and I arrived to the dorm room, my new roommate showed up. She was from New York and she was very nice, initially that is.... I don't recall meeting her mother, but I remember how anxious she was to choose her side of our room even though I had already claimed a bed. I remember thinking this is going to be an interesting experience sharing space with a stranger. However, she was very polite to my mother, so I thought to myself, "I'll be ok". I walked my mom to her car and we hugged and kissed goodbye as she begrudgingly left to go to the airport heading back to California. My mother is definitely not the affectionate type, so I knew when she hugged AND kissed me she was really nervous and worried about leaving me behind to start a new life so far away from her. I assured her and my Dad I would stay in touch once a week, so there was no need to worry.

AS SOON AS MY MOM LEFT THE BUILDING, MY NEW ROOMMATE COULDN'T WAIT TO TELL ME ABOUT THE PARTIES THAT WERE HAPPENING DURING THE FIRST WEEK OF SCHOOL.

She already had a few friends that were also new to Howard and she wanted me to meet them all. We went to a Freshman Orientation event, where we were introduced to our campus mentors, known as Campus Pals. Our campus pals gave us great advice about navigating our way through our first year by letting us know of great organizations to consider joining and great resource centers that would be available on campus to help us with our studies. I was very thankful to have a campus pal because she became someone I could call on when I was unsure about a lot of things both academically and socially.

As the year progressed, living with a new roommate definitely had its advantages and disadvantages. We had to really take the time to get to know each other, which meant there would be a few days when we just simply didn't get along. I remember my roommate telling me that she wanted to have friends over really late and that on occasion she may have a boyfriend come over. I told her I didn't mind as long as she told me ahead of time, so I could make plans to go somewhere quiet if I needed to study or if she needed private time with her guests. I asked that she extend me the same courtesy. She agreed and everything seemed to be fine until the day she and her friends decided to pull a practical joke on me.

One afternoon, I came home to the dorm to get some things for a rehearsal in class and discovered all of my stuff was removed from the room. I mean everything was gone! My bed was stripped of its sheets, my clothes were no longer in the closet, my portable stereo and my hot plate were all gone too! My entire side of the room looked as bare as it did when I moved in. I couldn't believe it. My roommate heard me enter the room and came from across the hall to say, "What happened? I can't believe somebody stole your stuff! What are you gonna do?" I knew immediately she was involved by the crooked smile on her face and the fact that she was conveniently just across the hall in another room with her friends hanging out while our door was left wide open. I was speechless for about 3 seconds and I just looked at her and said, "Everybody loves a good joke, but this is not cool. I gotta go to rehearsal and I hope all my stuff is back in my room just as it was when I get back". My roommate said, "I have no idea what you're talking about" as she tried to control her laughter. Slowly but surely, her friends from across the hall came over to see what was going on. They were all trying to stop themselves from laughing too.

I REPEATED OUT LOUD TO EVERYONE WHO CAME IN AND PEEKED AT MY ROOM, "I HOPE ALL MY STUFF IS BACK IN MY ROOM WHEN I GET BACK."

As I walked out of my room and passed each girl who came to see what was going on, I looked at everyone in the eye one at a time, grabbed my bag by the door and headed back to class rehearsal. While walking away, my roommate snickered and said, "What are you gonna do? Call the RA?" I simply replied, "Nope. She'll probably take too long to figure out who did it. See ya later." With that, I smiled and left them to stand there thinking about what I planned to do and who I would call. When I got outside, I was so angry because I didn't know why I was chosen to be picked on and I didn't have the things I needed for my rehearsal. I decided to remain calm because I remember dealing with a class bully in high school. Every time I tried to confront him about a disagreement or spoke up for myself, he would simply deny, deny, deny ANY wrongdoing. So this time in college, I decided to be silent and let the girls consider what I might do. Of course, there was one natural conclusion they may have considered, "If she doesn't call the RA, she'll probably call campus security or even worse, the police." I left them there to contemplate. I didn't say a thing. Somehow in my gut, I knew my stuff would be back in my room. I just had a feeling they knew they went too far.

When I left, I decided to call my cousin, Sandy who was also a freshman attending Howard at the same time. I told her about the incident and needless to say, she was just as pissed off as I was. She told me she wanted to pay me a visit just to make her presence known. She wanted the girls to know that I was not alone, and didn't mind letting them know in her own special way. I was completely distraught and didn't know what she meant, but she made me laugh and I was glad to know I had some family support nearby.

A few hours later, I returned back from my rehearsal and wouldn't you know it, my cousin, Sandy showed up to see me with some of her friends. I remember leaving the door open, so the girls in the hall could see me with my visitors. Sandy asked me to point out all the girls who were involved in taking my stuff. As the girls passed my room, I pointed a few of them out to my cousin. The girls appeared nervous and shocked to see my cousin and her friends.

Sandy noticed how distraught and embarrassed I was and she asked me to take a little walk and give her some time to talk with the girls in the dorm. Sandy brought her friends with her and I certainly hoped that her "talk with the girls" would not involve fighting the girls. I looked at Sandy and she looked at me. She knew I didn't want any trouble. With a nod of her head, she motioned for me to

go and assured me not to worry about anything.

I don't remember how long I was gone. But when I returned, Sandy and her friends were not there and everything on my side of the room was back in its place! I couldn't believe it! What did Sandy and her friends say to those girls? My roommate and about 3 of her friends came in to the room from across the hall to apologize. I just looked at them and said, "Thanks for returning my stuff. I'd appreciate it if you save the jokes for somebody else. I needed some things earlier and because of you guys I didn't have them." The girls really looked shocked that I was so pissed, yet so calm. But, I'm sure none of them would've appreciated the joke if the shoe were on the other foot. I snickered inside because I knew my cousin, Sandy and her friends left a serious impression on those girls!

Later that evening, one of my roommate's friends came over to personally apologize and tell me how much she respected the fact that I didn't panic and call the RA. She never told me what Sandy and her friends said to her, but she felt bad about the whole thing the moment she saw my face when I looked at my empty side of the room. To my surprise, she and I continued talking that evening and my anger about the whole day slowly began to disappear.

This was the first time I could recall any person of my age taking full responsibility for their actions. My cousin may have influenced her, but she still reached out to me for friendship instead of more ridicule and I never forgot that day. In fact, she and I became really good friends. I thought my roommate and I would have the close friendship, but instead I found a real friendship in one of her friends.

This did not go over well with my roommate. Eventually, her jealousy about my relationship with her friend began to bother her because all of her friends had now become people I didn't mind hanging out with. Needless to say, my relationship with my roommate started to become more and more uncomfortable. So, I asked the RA to move me to another dorm room. My RA had heard rumblings of the tension and agreed to move me. I still remained friends with many of the girls that year and my roommate ended up leaving Howard all together.

HONOR YOURSELF
Living away from home certainly proved to be another risk worth taking. I was ready to create new memories and soak up what HU had to offer, but I didn't know that living with a stranger would give me the opportunity to really see what I was made of. Unfortunately, I had a roommate who was not too comfortable with the idea of sharing space. However, I knew why I came to Howard and I wasn't gonna let anything get in the way of me enjoying my time there. I decided to give myself a chance to grow and prosper in this new world. I owed it to myself and all the people who helped me get to that point. Ultimately, this roommate experience proved to be a small, yet important bump in the road that reminded me to stay focused and remember why I was there.

BE FEARLESS
I also learned a little something about myself. As I stood amongst a group of girls, who were in on a practical joke at my expense, I noticed I didn't feel nervous or intimidated around them. I was angry and embarrassed, but I somehow knew to calm myself down after taking a few deep breaths, so that I would "never let them see me sweat" in that moment. As I defended myself, I began to

feel a sense of pride about the way I handled myself. I was also incredibly thankful to my cousin, Sandy for being there for me when I needed her. Clearly, I had learned from my high school experience that arguing back and forth probably wouldn't get me the result I was looking for. At the end of the day, I felt like respect was all I really needed and wanted from any of those girls. It no longer mattered to me why it happened.

ACCEPT RESPONSIBILITY

I admired the one girl who came to see me separately to apologize because she actually took responsibility for her actions. I was willing to be disliked, if it meant I was respected. But, this girl wanted to take the time to apologize and get to know me. I didn't even try to fit in with the group and I found out by being honest in the moment and taking responsibility for my feelings, I gained respect and a new friend in the process.

BE INVINCIBLE!

FOOD FOR THOUGHT

Focus

Can you remember a time when you were harassed by someone in school? How did you handle it?

_____

_____

_____

What do you do now to make sure no one takes your focus away from what you want to accomplish?

_____

_____

_____

Friendships

Is it more important for you to be liked and/or respected by others? Why?

_____

_____

_____

Do you have friends in your life that are honest with you about their feelings? Do you feel comfortable being honest with your friends about your feelings? Why or why not?

_____

_____

_____

The **Back to Me** Devotional

Chapter 4

ON MY WAY HOME

> "Some people succeed because they are destined to, but most people succeed because they are determined to." **Roscoe Dunjee**

> "On my way home, I wanna hear Him say, 'Well done'."
> **On My Way Home Lyric from my 'Back to Me' Album**

> "For the revelation awaits an appointed time; it speaks of the end and will not prove false. Though it linger, wait on it; it will certainly come and will not delay." **Habakkuk 2:3 NIV**

A CHANCE MEETING WITH DESTINY

My freshman year as a Musical Theatre major was full of incredible opportunities to meet amazing guest speakers and Howard Alumni actors, who had gone on to receive critical acclaim and major success in the entertainment industry. One of the first speakers I remember visiting my theatre class was Avery Brooks. When I heard that Hawk from the popular television series, "Spencer for Hire" was coming to visit us, I couldn't wait to meet the tall, dark, and handsome man with the unmistakable deep voice that used to keep me tuned in every week to watch his show. My Dad was also a professional actor and he

used to tell me, "Nobody could play Paul Robeson on the theatre stage better than Avery Brooks". So, I was even more excited to call home and tell him that the Hawk...I mean Mr. Brooks was coming to talk to my class!

Before he came into our class, my professor gave us a brief summary of who he was and listed some of his accomplishments. Many of us already knew who he was and were getting very anxious for him to walk through the door. When he finally entered the auditorium where our class was being held, we immediately applauded and couldn't wait to hear what he had to say. He greeted us with "Hello, Everyone!" in that magical and distinct voice of his. He began to thank us and tell us what a privilege it was for him to meet us as well. I remember smiling ear to ear with my face in my hands and my elbows on my knees sitting at the edge of my seat waiting to hear what we wanted to tell us about being an actor.

Mr. Brooks was very warm and giving as he shared a few stories about his journey through theatre and television. I was so grateful to get a glimpse of what my life could be like as a performing artist, and not a celebrity seeking fame, which he frowned upon greatly. He was the first person to help me realize that acting and theatre performance was an art form to be taken seriously. It was our responsibility to handle our characters carefully and offer them our truest intention, so we could be fully available to them in the most powerful way possible. Many other speakers came to visit us Among them were the beloved Academy award nominated actress and playwright, Ruby Dee, her husband, the NAACP Image and American Theater Hall of Fame award recipient, Ossie Davis, as well as Tony award actress, Phylicia Rashad, known to so many as one of America's favorite TV moms, Ms. Claire Huxtable from the "Cosby Show", just to name a few. These incredibly generous actors taught us to embody and feel every character we played with every fiber of our being. Interpreting a character was one thing, but becoming the character in all of its glory was quite another.

I learned about the honesty of acting and the importance of staying true to the integrity of my characters. It was emotionally draining work, but we became so disciplined about our craft in the process. Every part, big or small was important and relevant. Every character on the stage had a story and we were to figure it out and bring their magic to life whether we spoke a scripted line or not. I fell in love with the process and I loved how it all made me feel about being vulnerable and available on stage. Slowly, but surely the stage was becoming my true "home away from home". I loved being there. I was always nervous when called upon, but I loved the therapy I received in that space everyday.

 MY CLASSMATES AND I BECAME A FAMILY. WE LOOKED AFTER EACH OTHER. WE LEARNED TO NURTURE OUR CHARACTERS AND THEREFORE NURTURE EACH OTHER.

I never thought I'd connect so quickly with such amazingly talented people. Our professors became our surrogate parents and we were their cherished children. They kept tabs on us during and after school hours. The pursuit of excellence was a must and we were to represent

ourselves as such at all times.

The day Ms. Rashad came to speak to us, I was surprised to learn that her sister and my TV mentor, Debbie Allen was actually in the building too!! She was speaking in another class. I thought it was a joke, but one of my classmates said she was just down the hall. The thought of Ms. Lydia Grant from the television series, "Fame" being just down the hall gave me chills and my heart leaped with uncontrollable excitement. I was merely a few feet away from meeting the woman who inspired me to come to Howard in the first place! The idea of actually meeting her never crossed my mind. Even as I sat and listened to her sister, Ms. Rashad, I never thought Ms. Allen would also be there too, and on the same day!!!

MY MIND FLASHED BACK TO THE LINE IN "FAME" SHE MADE FAMOUS, "YOU WANT FAME? WELL FAME COSTS AND RIGHT HERE IS WHERE YOU START PAYING...IN SWEAT."

I was sweating alright. The idea of getting an opportunity to meet and possibly speak to her had me sweating! My high school dance teacher, Ka-Ron Lehman was my own version of Ms. Lydia Grant. Ka-Ron was firm and she pushed my classmates and I to be the best dancers we could be, while loving on us like no teacher I had ever had before. She still loves on me today and I'm so thankful to have her in my life. Ms. Lydia Grant was my TV mentor, but Ms. Ka-Ron Lehman was my real mentor and she made the idea of Ms. Grant real for me in my life.

And now I was about to meet the actual woman who brought Ms. Grant to life! It was too much to handle. I remember getting up to use the restroom while we had a break from Ms. Rashad's workshop. As I walked to the restroom, guess who came right out? Yep!! Debbie Allen herself. I didn't believe my eyes. I was walking toward her and all I was thinking was "That can't be her. That can't be her. What should I say? I can't say anything. I might sound like a crazed fan. This is a working environment, and I need to be respectful, and not turn into a groupie. I want to tell her so badly that she's the reason I'm here... Oh no! Here she comes." As Ms. Allen passed me, I could only say. "Hello, Ms. Allen." She looked at me with a comforting smile and said, "Hi, baby". And with that, she was gone and went back into the classroom she came from. I stood in the hallway dumbfounded. Why didn't I tell her she inspired me to be there? I was so mad at myself. The shock of it all took over me and I missed my chance. I was hoping I'd see her again that day, but she was gone and my opportunity to thank her for all she had done to inspire me to get this far was gone too.

But, somehow I knew I would get another chance one day and I would be better prepared to express myself without all of the excitement and nerves overshadowing our conversation. So, I decided that day that I would continue to learn my craft and do everything it would take to be my best. I was gonna pay with my sweat and someday get another opportunity to tell her, " Thank you."

TAKE YOUR ART FORM SERIOUSLY

Although I did not choose Musical Theatre as my major initially, I was so glad I was open to explore this major and all it had to offer. As a Theatre major, I'm sure

I would have met some of the same speakers, but I learned through constant rehearsal and vocal classes that my voice was not only an instrument of song, but also an instrument of social change. I fell in love with the idea that I had the unique ability to bring life and clarity through song to my characters, in a way that soothed the soul melodically, and penetrated the heart spiritually. Everyday my purpose became clearer and I knew my voice would take me somewhere. I was becoming more than an actor, more than a singer, I was becoming a healer because of the way I was being taught to introduce my characters on stage.

ENJOY THE PROCESS

Between show rehearsals and classes, I rarely saw my dorm room. I was fully engaged in learning all I could about my craft. My professors and classmates had become my new family members, and I didn't wanna miss a thing. I knew this experience would stay with me for the rest of my life. So, I relished in the laughter we shared together, the tears we shed from giving our all and leaving it on the stage, to the discipline we received from our professors to remain focused. Often times, I did not think Professor M liked me very much. I knew he saw something special in me during my audition interview, but I wasn't sure if he liked me. He was not an affectionate man, but the time and energy he put into directing all of us assured me of his commitment to transform us into the incredible performers he knew we were becoming.

PREPARE FOR YOUR OPPORTUNITY

Coming face to face with my television mentor and the reason I came to Howard, startled me in ways I never imagined. Who knew I would freeze up when I got the chance to meet her? Why was I so scared to just release all that I was feeling in that one moment? I believe it was because I was not prepared for that moment. I had not yet paid the cost or sweated enough to fully appreciate and understand the value of that moment. But, I knew I would never let an opportunity like that come again and I not be prepared. So, it's quite possible that the moment actually served its purpose. Running into the person who inspired me for so long, reminded me to keep moving forward because I must've been on the right path and in the right place, if she was on it with me at the same time. Sometimes, a chance meeting with destiny is an encounter that will shape the rest of your life. Learn from it and when given the chance to meet again, speak up and...

DON'T MISS YOUR OPPORTUNITY!

The **Back to Me** Devotional

FOOD FOR THOUGHT

College Major
Are you serious about the college major you have chosen? If so, what do you love about it?

_____
_____
_____
_____
_____
_____

If not, what is preventing you from pursuing a major you really love?

_____
_____
_____

Lessons and Opportunities
What lessons have you already learned about yourself during your college experience?

_____
_____
_____
_____

What opportunities are you currently preparing for?

_____
_____
_____

Chapter 5

ANYBODY OUT THERE?

"But love is blind and lovers cannot see the pretty follies that themselves commit..." – William Shakespeare from his play, **'The Merchant of Venice'**

"Show up with confidence, intelligence, then I'll be ready to share with you my world." **Anybody Out There Lyric from my 'Back to Me' Album**

"...Love your neighbor as yourself. There is no commandment greater than these." **Mark 12:31 NIV**

WHEN LOVE IS BLIND

My developing love for the arts wasn't the only thing that kept my blood racing. I met a guy in the Fine Arts Dept., who was a musician. He was older and he had been at Howard a couple years already. He was very friendly, polite, did I say "older"?, and he thought I was an amazing talent. He often made it a point to call me to check on me to see how I was doing. We used to talk for hours on the phone. He was attentive, I thought. But, my friends thought he was a little too attentive. On many occasions, they wanted me to hang out with them, but I had already

made plans to hang out with him. They hated it. They were beginning to think I didn't want to be with them because I was beginning to spend so much time with him. I tried to assure them that I would make it up the following week, but day-by-day, they got tired of waiting on me.

Before I knew it, I found myself spending most available weekends with him. I enjoyed talking to him about music and he introduced me to some of the best local supper clubs in DC. He would sometimes perform with his musician friends at one of the clubs that soon became my favorite, TJ Remington's. I loved that place. There was an energy in that place that was undeniable. It was a restaurant, so college students were allowed and I got to see how the older crowd lived after hours!! The live music, the beautiful people in their evening attire, and the amazing food was all very intoxicating to me. I loved the connection the featured singer and the musicians had with the people. It was slightly different than what I was learning on the theatrical stage, but it was just as exciting to watch.

My new boyfriend and I were now getting a little more serious, and one of the major things that kept me interested in him was being able to go to the supper club! He exposed me to a whole new world outside of college and I couldn't wait to get a chance to possibly sing with the live band. I loved going to learn from the various singers that were there on different nights. If I wasn't singing in the Fine Arts building at Howard, I wanted to be singing in one of those clubs.

As the year progressed, my boyfriend went from being a musician that occasionally played at TJ Remington's to being a featured act there! He asked me if I still wanted to sing at the club, and I screamed, "Yes! When?" He told me I needed to learn a few tunes, from artists like, Anita Baker, Mary J. Blige, and Chaka Khan. I grew up listening to their music and I told him, "I already know their songs. Which ones do you want?" Within a couple weeks, I was given my first opportunity to sing to a live audience of adults that were not my peers in school. I couldn't believe it. I was extremely nervous, but I knew I could do it. It was time to put some of what I'd been learning in class to use in front of a real audience. I wanted to see if I could move them the way I was able to move some of my peers in our show rehearsals.

The evening finally came and it was time to sing one of the songs I had rehearsed with the band. I chose "Sweet Thing" by Chaka Khan as my opener.

 AS SOON AS THE CROWD HEARD THE FIRST FEW NOTES IN THE SONG FROM THE GUITARIST, THEY WERE SHOUTING, "AHH, YEAH!! THAT'S MY JAM! COME ON, GIRL! BRING IT!"

I started to sing the first line, "I will love you anyway..." and they shouted again, "Alright now!" I continued, "Even if you cannot stay. I think you are the one for me. Here is where you want to be..." The crowd loved it and I loved singing those words! I started thinking about how I was taught to bring life to the words and deliver the moment from my professors. The moment was real for me and I meant every word. "Whoa, oh, sweet thing. Don't ya know you're my everything!..." As I sang, I glanced over to my boyfriend, who was on the bass. He looked at me as if I was singing to him. But, I realized in that same moment that I was singing to Music. I was singing to the Experience. I was in love and it had nothing to do with my boyfriend. I was in love with Music and I know Music was in love with me!!! I could feel it! I knew I would be doing this for the rest of my life!

When the show ended, many people came to congratulate me and they encouraged me to keep singing. They made me feel so special. I was so thankful to my boyfriend and he was excited for me too. He invited me to perform a few more times and I thoroughly enjoyed it. I was now able to take some of the skills I had been developing in the supper club to the theatrical stage.

Performing on stage at school and performing in the supper club became a routine for me. I was fully immersed in my craft and I felt like the luckiest girl in the world. To hone in on my craft even more, my boyfriend and I would also go see some incredible female recording artists at the Blues Alley. This supper club was and still is the hottest spot for live jazz entertainment that is on another level! I saw jazz vocalist and songwriter, Cassandra Wilson. Her deep voice mesmerized me on stage and my locs today were inspired by her beautiful golden locs. She was so regal to me and I couldn't take my eyes off of her. Then one night, we saw Phyllis Hyman. This was a special treat for me because I have always adored her voice. The passion and pain that came through whenever she sang was unmatched. I was so excited to see her.

Until one day, my boyfriend started to feel like I was losing interest in him. I was starting to miss my friends and I realized that I had given so much of my time to music and him that I forgot about my friends. I told him that I wanted to take a break. He assumed that meant I wanted to date other people, I didn't mean that at the time, but as he started to show an angry, jealous side that I had not seen before, I thought maybe it was a good idea. After all, my Dad was also nervous about me spending too much time with a boyfriend he never met and he was the only person I had dated for much of my college experience. I felt I needed to be free to explore other relationships without him feeling left out.

Our relationship slowly started to unravel by my senior year. He did not finish his studies at Howard and he went on to work as a restaurant manager in the city. I was performing more and more with my colleagues in school, and I was surprised to feel like a heavy weight of judgment and responsibility had lifted when my boyfriend left Howard.

I am so thankful to him for exposing me to another magical world of music that I might not have ever known if we didn't meet. But, I discovered that love is a funny thing. It can take you on a wild ride that can cause you to leave everything behind just to have the chance to experience it or it can help you discover things about yourself you never knew existed.

BROADEN YOUR HORIZONS
I don't regret the ride, because it taught me to value all of my relationships without compromising one for the other. When I met my boyfriend, I got caught up in a whirlwind of romantic weekends and endless phone

calls. I loved the attention, and didn't really feel like I was missing much because I was always surrounded by music. After all, music turned out to be the one thing I truly fell in love with. But, meeting new and exciting people was also important. I limited my experience and myself by spending too much available time with one person.

BE CAREFUL WITH INTIMACY

Those romantic weekends and endless phone calls were fun, but came with the price of missed opportunities to be with friends. In a dating relationship, getting to know someone is a very intimate and beautiful thing. But, it can cause you to want to share some of the most private things about yourself and your body too soon. It can also mislead you into believing the relationship means more than it actually does. Be careful. Intimacy can be distracting and it can keep someone that you do not really know in your life longer than you anticipated.

IDENTIFY A HEALTHY DATING RELATIONSHIP

If you do find a love interest while in college, take time out to identify what you really expect from someone who claims to love you. It can start with you defining what you love about yourself. Consider everything from your academic success to your friendship/family values to your spiritual compatibility. Be on the look out for someone who confirms those things about you, and represents those things in themselves. Be safe and go out on group dates initially to see how this person responds to your friends and how your friends respond back. Beware of predators disguised as a great "catch" because of their popularity or academic reputation. You don't want to be considered "fresh meat". So, remember why you came to school in the first place, surround yourself with people who positively challenge you and cheer you on, and protect the integrity of all your relationships by treating them with the unique respect they all deserve.

LOVE YOURSELF MORE

If you discover it is time to move on from a dating relationship that no longer serves you, don't be afraid to speak up and say so. Remember to be respectful, but love yourself enough to speak up and choose what you believe is best for you. College is a once in a lifetime experience. Don't waste it on regret.

CHOOSE YOU EVERY TIME!

FOOD FOR THOUGHT

Dating
Have you ever given so much of your time to a dating partner that it sacrificed some of your friendships? If so, do you think it was worth it?

_____
_____
_____
_____
_____

Do you believe sexual intimacy can cloud your judgment in a relationship? Why or why not?

_____
_____
_____
_____

Personal Standards
Describe the top 10 things you love about yourself. Describe the top 10 things you need to be happy. In your life, who acknowledges and honors these things about you?

_____
_____
_____
_____

Have you ever had to walk away from a dating relationship? If so, how did you feel afterward? If not, how did you feel when the person left you?

_____
_____
_____
_____

Chapter 6

SO BEAUTIFUL

"We all have to escape from this thing called life sometimes. Maybe we use substances to do it. Maybe we use religion. Maybe we use exercise. Maybe we use anger. But we all have to do it. 'How' we do it is what defines us." **Dan Pearce**

"When I close my eyes, all I can see is me and you. And when our worlds collide, it could be so beautiful."
So Beautiful Lyric from my 'Back to Me' Album

"Be alert and of sober mind. Your enemy the devil prowls around like a roaring lion looking for someone to devour." **1 Peter 5:8 NIV**

SMOKE AND MIRRORS

Even though much of my free time was spent in the Fine Arts building or at the supper club, I did manage to find time to hang out with my friends from my dorm. Back at the dorm, there was always excitement in the hallways. Most of us kept our doors open, so we could talk to one another from across the hall. We could also hear which room was hosting the best party before curfew. Fortunately, I was always directly across the hall from one of the cool rooms with great music and fun card games.

When my "roommate from hell" left Howard, I was able to have my room to myself for the rest of the year. I was really happy about that because I was able to practice my lines from school musicals without having to leave my room. I was also able to host game parties as well without worrying about disturbing my roommate. Our card games were so much fun too. I got really good at playing Spades and Uno.

One weekend, a few of my friends in the dorm came to my room to invite me to a fraternity party they heard about near campus. I was tired and bored that evening, so I agreed to go. The fraternity house was walking distance from our dorm. I was excited to get off campus with my friends, and I felt safe enough to go because the party wasn't too far away from our dorm.

When we got there, the house was full of college students having a great time. I remember the lights being low and plenty of folks dancing with each other, while holding their red plastic cups of Ever Clear punch. I had never heard of Ever Clear punch before, but I was told it was an alcohol that you could hardly taste in the punch. So, my friends and I went over to the refreshment table where the punch bowl was and filled up our cups! After about 30 minutes, I started to really feel drowsy. I was sillier than usual. For some reason, everything was funny to me. Guys were starting to notice me and my friends now. A few of them came over to find out who we were and what was so funny. We told them we were new to Howard. I recognized one of the guys from the Fine Arts Dept. and we struck up a conversation, while the other guys started talking to my friends. These guys were cute, but my head was starting to hurt and I was starting to feel sick. One of my friends yelled out, "Light weight!

What's wrong? You ok?" I told her I was ok, but I was feeling like I was going to pass out. I didn't want them or the guy talking to me to think I couldn't hang with the best of them. So, I quietly excused myself and slowly made my way back to the refreshment table, while holding onto to the wall to get some water to wake myself up.

When I got to the table this time, there was another guy there in a big black jacket. It was pretty hot in the house from all the body heat and I thought it was strange that he was still wearing his jacket. He didn't really seem happy to be there, but he did acknowledge me with a nod of his head when I walked over. He actually looked sad and I asked him if he was having a good time. He said, "I'm alright." I told him, "I'm not. That punch was too much for me." He said, "Yeah. You gotta take your time with that stuff. Drink some water. You'll be alright." I thought to myself, for a guy who seemed to be bored with the whole night, he was pretty cool. So, I stayed at the punch table for awhile and just began to watch the crowd with him. No words were spoken. We were just watching the crowd. I could see my friends still talking and dancing with the same guys, so I figured they wouldn't notice me trying to recover from that punch by drinking water.

After a few songs had played, I noticed the quiet, but sad guy next to me in the hot jacket had moved away. He made his way to the center of the dance floor and started yelling out something nobody could understand over the music. So, everybody just kept dancing. I thought it was strange that he was yelling for no apparent reason, but I was too dizzy to even try and comprehend what he was saying. Besides, by that time someone had lit up a joint and you could smell the marijuana in the air. So, I was not only dizzy, but I was starting to feel really relaxed without a care in the world. My head was still hurting a

little, but I didn't seem to mind as much anymore because that marijuana had me feeling like a beautiful bird about to take flight.

A few minutes later, the guy in the jacket yelled out again, but no one said a thing or paid him any attention. Between the Go-go music, the weed, and the punch that was constantly being passed around, everybody was feeling pretty good. I was starting to enjoy myself, but something told me I needed to get outta there before I passed out and woke up somewhere I wasn't supposed to. So, I made my way back over to my friends to tell them I was gonna head back to the dorm and they should probably come with me.

ONE OF MY FRIENDS SAID, "YOU PARTY POOPER! I THOUGHT YOU SAID YOU WERE OK." I TOLD HER, "I AM, BUT.." JUST AS I WAS ABOUT TO TELL HER ABOUT THE STRANGE GUY YELLING IN THE BLACK JACKET, 2 SHOTS RANG OUT!

At first, nobody stopped dancing because the music was so loud and it wasn't clear what it was. Then, another shot rang out! This time I could hear a girl scream and everybody started to run out of the house. The lights came on, the music stopped and there he was, the guy in the black jacket pointing a gun at someone he just shot in the leg. I screamed and my friends and I ran outta there as fast we could. I couldn't believe that I was just talking to a guy who came specifically to the party to shoot somebody!! What?? He seemed so nice, sad, but nice. As we ran the whole way back to the dorm, my heart was beating so fast. Suddenly the cool air, sobered all of us right up!! I was so scared the guy was gonna come after me because I spent time with him and knew what he looked like. I was praying so hard, "Lord, Please don't let this guy come looking for me."

When we got back to the dorm, one of my friends called the police. I was shaking and too scared to do anything. I didn't wanna leave my room for the rest of the weekend. I couldn't believe what just happened. A night that started off with so much excitement quickly turned into chaos in the blink of an eye.

The next day, the shooting was on the news and to our surprise, none of the police officers came to our dorm to question us. We didn't tell the RA that we went to the party that night. We just wanted to forget we were even there. None of us got any sleep that night either. I was still so worried about the shooter coming to look for me, but someone in the dorm heard it was a gang related shooting by someone from the Southeast area of DC. The police had an idea about the gangs in that area and turned their focus away from our school. Hearing that news made me feel a little better, but I wanted somebody to escort me to the Fine Arts building for the next week, just in case.

A few days later, the Fine Arts student I recognized at the party told me the police found the shooter. I was so glad to hear that. I decided that day that would be the last fraternity house party I went to for awhile. That was enough excitement for me.

BE CAREFUL WITH BOREDOM

You never know where boredom will take you. I was ready to get out and have fun with my friends at my first frat party. But, I had no idea what would be waiting for me when I got there. I love to have a good time and I encourage you to do the same. But, be sure to take a few friends with you and try to go to a party where at least one of your friends knows a fraternity brother. Stay close to your friends, leave with your friends, and more than likely you'll be safe and create some wonderful memories.

RECOGNIZE PEER PRESSURE

The moment we walked in the door, the groove of the music and the joy in the atmosphere made us feel right at home. Everyone was dancing and everyone was so friendly. I wanted to experience some of that joy and if it meant drinking some Ever Clear punch, I was in! But, I didn't expect it to affect me the way it did. When my friends teased me about my "light weight" status, it did make me wanna prove them wrong. Fortunately, my instincts told me to stop and get some water. So, before you attempt to prove something to someone in order to fit in, check in with yourself and make sure your decisions are your own and that those decisions benefit you in the end.

BEWARE OF THAT ALTERED STATE OF MIND

Drugs have a way of tricking the mind to believe all is well. But when they wear off, life is right where you left it. The smell of marijuana may have taken me to a higher place, but I was losing control and I didn't like that feeling. Whenever school or other people made me feel stressed and in need of an escape, I learned to soothe my soul and transport my mind with music, journaling, and guided meditation. Alter your mind with these ideas, and you'll always be able to manage the highs and lows of your life.

BREATHING AND MEDITATION EXERCISES

Breathing Exercise: Make yourself comfortable by sitting up in a chair or lying down. Get still and notice how your stomach rises when you inhale and settles when you exhale. Take in a deep breath through your nose forcing the air to the back of your throat for 4 counts. Hold the air for 4 counts. Then release the air through your mouth for 4 counts. Repeat at least three times and notice how your heart rate slows and your body starts to relax. Do this whenever you feel overwhelmed.

Meditation Exercise: Sit up in a chair or lie down for this exercise too. Light your favorite scented candle or massage your favorite scented oil into your skin. Peppermint and Lavender oils are my favorites! You can search YouTube.com for some soothing instrumental meditative music or you can choose silence. Close your eyes. Complete the breathing exercise above and visualize three things you want to achieve this year. See yourself achieving these things and notice how the thrill of accomplishment makes you feel. Try to hold that feeling for five to ten minutes. Allow yourself to be thankful for the accomplishment. Think of what you did to get there. After five or ten minutes, say to yourself, "I am..." Complete the statement or mantra with a word or feeling that came up for you during your visualization. Repeat that statement for one more minute. After one minute, slowly move your body. Stretch your arms and legs. Open your eyes and remind yourself of your statement throughout your day or your evening, if you choose to do this to help you sleep.

FREE YOUR MIND!

The **Back to Me** Devotional

FOOD FOR THOUGHT

Solitude
Do you have to be around people to have fun? Why or
why not?

_____

_____

_____

Do you listen to your own instincts or do you tend to
follow the crowd?

_____

_____

_____

Stress Release
What do you like to do to release stress and escape your
reality?

_____

_____

_____

Chapter 7

BACK TO ME

"Our deepest fear is not that we are inadequate. Our deepest fear is that we are powerful beyond measure. It is our light, not our darkness, that most frightens us...
And as we let our own lights shine, we unconsciously give other people permission to do the same." **Marianne Williamson**

"When you're feelin' lost and you're all alone, realize all you need is yourself." **Back to Me Lyric from my 'Back to Me' Album**

"The Lord is my light and my salvation-whom shall I fear? The Lord is the stronghold of my life-of whom shall I be afraid?" **Psalm 27:1 NIV**

BECOMING A DREAMGIRL

My identity as a young woman and a performing artist began to take shape in my junior year. I was becoming more and more comfortable with stage direction from my mentor, Professor M. and I was no longer intimidated by his correction. I was beginning to understand why he had pushed me and my colleagues so hard. He saw something great in all of us and he refused to let up until he got what he wanted from us. He knew how to identify our unique abilities and bring out the best in us to make

all of our lights shine.

 ONE OF OUR GREATEST OPPORTUNITIES TO SHINE CAME WHEN WE WERE CAST IN DREAMGIRLS!

This Tony Award and Academy Award winning Broadway musical and feature film did not only impact audiences around the world in the 80s and later in its 2006 movie version, but I would argue to say our 1992 Howard University production garnered critical acclaim as well.

The Fine Arts building was full of anticipation about who would be cast in what role. Professor M was the director and he told us this production was going to be one of the best and it would require dedication from the best. Therefore, the audition process was going to be intense and there was no room for half-stepping or showing up unprepared. He wanted Howard's musical interpretation of this well-respected play to be unforgettable and special. So, we knew going in that our best was required or we would quickly be replaced. It was time to put on my big girl pants and show him that I was ready.

The audition process was long and the emotional roller coaster I found myself on seemed liked it would never end. But, by the end of the week, I found out I won the role of Michelle Morris. I was selected to play the Dreamgirl who would eventually replace the main character, Effie White in the singing group. What? I was selected to be a Dreamgirl?? Whoa!! I thought I might get an understudy role as one of the characters, but never did I think I'd land an actual Dreamgirl role. I was excited, but terribly nervous. This was an honor and I wanted to bring my best performance to the role for Professor M and myself.

The character was a bit shy, but she had just enough sparkle and backbone to stand in the face of Effie White and make her presence known. In a strange way, I felt so connected to this character. I just went through a grueling, competitive audition process with a few naysayers watching on and I thought to myself, "Hey! Focus! You've been living this character for the past two years since you got here and you're still standing. So, go out there and show the people who Michelle is. Show them who you are!!" After psyching myself up, I suddenly realized that I was psyching myself up!! I told myself, "I can be anyone I choose to be. Right now, I am Michelle Morris! I'm a Dreamgirl!" Somewhere deep inside me, I was finally beginning to empower myself despite my fears. For the first time in my life, I didn't need a pep talk from anyone. I usually had my parents, my high school dance teacher, or my friends to help convince me I could do something. But this time, I encouraged myself and it felt good. As nervous as I was to be singing as a trio next to some of the best voices in our department, I decided to just show up and let God do the rest. I was grateful for the chance to prove myself and I wasn't going to waste it.

To calm my nerves somewhat, I began to practice every step and master every vocal part before, during, and after school. The mirror became my best friend. I remember staying after school waiting for the dance room to clear out, so I could practice my dance moves, my stage presence, and my vocal parts every chance I could. I wanted to show up to rehearsals with this character in my system. This way any new direction from

Professor M would be effortless, and any remaining self-doubt would be gone. I had to live and breathe the character of Michelle, and I was determined to make it happen.

Rehearsals became more and more exciting for me because I was developing my own confidence and a sense resiliency for every hour we stayed after school to get the show just right. Every dance move and every vocal part was significant for every scene. I noticed my stamina had improved as well. We practiced our movement so much that not only was my mind being conditioned for greatness, but so was my body and spirit. There was no real need for exercise because we certainly got a workout in those rehearsals.

A month or so later, our premiere night arrived and the anticipation of giving the audience a great show was all we could think about. All the hard work was finally going to pay off. The moment the lights went up and the first song rang out, the audience was cheering! I knew we had them. It was just up to us to keep the momentum going and take the audience on the most entertaining ride of their lives.

Song after song, and one phenomenal performance after another proved to be our best show of the season. Students and local residents alike talked about our show and many told us they came back a few times just to see it and experience it again!

We all wanted the show to be great and I grew so much more respect for my cast mates. We always knew we were a family, but somehow this show solidified our relationship for the rest of our lives. I knew when I left

Howard, I would be connected to these people forever. They became my inspiration to always support my fellow man, pursue excellence and be my very best.

I AM. I WILL. I AM GRATEFUL FOR...
By performing in this show, I learned to embrace all of my fears and carry them with me until they fell away and no longer served a purpose. All of the "peace stealing" thoughts that ran through my head motivated me to prove them wrong. I was determined to be my greatest encourager. I remembered all the encouraging words my teachers, family, and friends instilled in me and I empowered myself to succeed. I saw myself conquering my fear and I did. My mantra became I am a winner. I will succeed, and I am grateful for this moment. I encourage you to create your own mantra and watch yourself soar to heights you may have never thought possible.

GET COMFORTABLE WITH THE FEELING OF PEACE
When I decided to stay after school and practice until I felt I had mastered the role of Michelle in my system, I never thought I had the discipline to do so. I just knew I didn't want to embarrass myself, my cast or my professor. But those after school practice sessions brought me a level of peace I didn't expect. I initially practiced with a great deal of stress and anxiety, but as I became comfortable with the movement and the songs, I found myself looking forward to these private moments of determination. When I got flustered, I stopped and soothed my mind with breathing exercises that slowed my heart and assured me all would be well. I figured out that by giving my all, it was enough and sufficient. I became the calm in my own storm and eventually my storm subsided.

NOURISH AND FUEL YOUR BODY
Stress and/or anxiety will always play a role in your life.

The key is to decide how you will use it to your advantage. How much control will you give it in your life? How long will you allow it to hang out in your mind and steal your peace? Pursuing things that interest you will help, but diet and exercise will support your effort to be at your best, both physically and mentally. Just the distraction of keeping up with the treadmill or walking a couple miles a day on campus will cause you to focus on your heart rate more than your problems. Nourish your mind with music and nourish your body with fresh squeezed juice, a high protein breakfast, and a fulfilling lunch of protein and veggies. When dinner rolls around, you can eat lighter and save room for fruit-based dessert. Eating this way will not only nourish your mind and body, but it will offer the fuel your body needs to be strong and ready to tackle any obstacle life tries to send your way.

SEEK INSPIRATION!

Fortunately, I chose a college major that fulfilled me mentally, spiritually, and physically. I encourage you to do the same. If you are still undecided about your major, try to participate in campus activities that peek your interest. I also found comfort in performing in the Howard Chorale because I enjoyed gospel music. My college counselor exposed me to community outreach opportunities as well. So, take care of your heart by finding out what makes your heart sing. Take care of your mind by supplying it with your own words of encouragement, and take care of your body because it is the one instrument that will carry you over your personal finish line and garner you the satisfaction you deserve.

BE SELF-ISH!

FOOD FOR THOUGHT

Distractions
Can you recall a time when you felt your peace was being taken away from you? What encouraging words kept you on track and focused on your goal?

_____

_____

_____

_____

Affirmations
Complete this mantra and repeat it daily when you wake up in the morning:
I am...
I will...
I am grateful for...

_____

_____

Wellness Plan
What does your daily diet and exercise plan consist of? (include breakfast, lunch, dinner, and your daily cardio routine) What activities inspire your mind, body and soul?

_____

_____

_____

_____

_____

_____

The **Back to Me** Devotional

HOLDING ON TO US

"Preservation of one's own culture does not require contempt or disrespect for other cultures" **Cesar Chavez**

"You don't have to fight all alone cuz when you're hurtin', I'm hurtin'."
Holding Onto Us Lyric from my 'Back to Me' Album

"I will instruct you and teach you in the way you should go; I will counsel you with my loving eye on you." **Psalm 32:8 NIV**

LIVING MY WILDEST DREAM

I can honestly say that everyday of my junior year brought me so much joy. Professor M was so proud of all of us for our hard work in the performance of 'Dreamgirls'. It was one of the few times I actually saw him smile with such pride for his students. He appeared to be 'flying on cloud nine' like the rest of us. I was so happy to know we put that beautiful smile on his face.

In the midst of all our excitement during that season, Professor M called the cast together to make a special announcement. We were all very anxious to know what could be more special than performing in one of the

most talked about musicals at Howard University. We all gathered together to hear what Professor M had to say. Many were rumbling about what they thought he might tell us. Some thought he was going to tell us our version of 'Dreamgirls' was gonna be held over again and extended for more shows. While others thought our show would get the opportunity to perform somewhere else in the city. The anticipation was killing me and I couldn't wait to find out what was really going on.

Professor M settled us all down and congratulated us yet again for our dedication and commitment to each and every character that walked across the stage. He told us he was proud of us and that our hard work had garnered the attention of some very special people. I couldn't wait. I thought, "Spit it out already!! What people?" He went on to say that we were invited to travel to Hong Kong, China to perform our version of 'Dreamgirls'!! What??? Hong, Kong, China?? Did he really just say that? We all screamed with excitement! No one could believe we were headed overseas, let alone China!! Wowwww! This was too much to handle! I had always thought about studying abroad and wondered if I would get that chance while at Howard. I loved the education I was receiving, but to travel abroad and learn about another culture was a chance in a lifetime and I couldn't wait to go!

 PREPARING TO PERFORM IN HONG KONG FELT SLIGHTLY DIFFERENT THAN PREPARING FOR ONE OF OUR SCHOOL PERFORMANCES.

My nerves were starting to creep back up again. I had

gotten comfortable with the stage and the intimacy of our audience in the Ira Aldridge Theater. I was not sure how another audience, let alone one of a different culture that didn't speak the same language would receive us. I told myself to trust the process and enjoy the ride. Something told me this was going to be an experience I'd never forget!

When we arrived in Hong Kong the weather was cold and it rained periodically, but it was a beautiful place to behold. The streets were busy like the pace of New York and the historical presence of Chinese art and culture was everywhere. I fell in love with the fast pace and the warm greetings we received. We were greeted by a group of Hong Kong Ambassadors who were very excited to see the show and us as well! After they told us briefly about our itinerary for the week, Professor M told us we would have a few days to rehearse and give them the best show possible.

During rehearsal, many of us started to get a little sick because of the weather change. We were worried about our performance and hoped our voices would carry us through. Professor M told us to take care of ourselves with plenty of hot liquids. But, he looked worried about us too. As a Dreamgirl, my group members and I were asked to perform for a special event prior to the show. We were cold and sick, but that day we learned the show must go on. So, we bundled up as best we could until performance time and then gave the small audience a taste of what they could expect during the show. Professor M was so proud of us for making it through that event. He knew we were tired, but we did it and we sounded great!

A few days later, we performed our first full show for the audience in a beautiful theatre and the people

loved it!! They didn't understand the language, but they connected to the music and the imagery our show had to offer just like the audiences did back home. It was amazing to see some of the emotion in their faces as they connected to the visual storyline. I knew then that the human experience and the power of music connected us all. I began to think how lucky we were to have had this experience.

After the show, the Ambassadors hosted a dinner for us and we were able to meet with some of the audience members. They were so gracious and kind. They thoroughly enjoyed us. Those that spoke English asked about our school and how long we had been performing the show. I was asked if I was a Music major and if I planned to continue singing as a profession. I was stunned by the question because it immediately made me think about how much more I enjoyed singing than acting. I responded and said, "I am a Musical Theatre major, but I think I will probably pursue singing more seriously. Who knows? You might see me back here someday!" I was thankful for the exchange because it told me I had something special that could possibly take me to places I had never dreamed of.

Never in my wildest dreams, did I think that this trip to study and perform abroad would help me learn more about myself, my cast mates, and how inspiring an international connection with others could be. As a result of this experience, my dream to perform around the world was being realized and it may have remained a dream had it not been for this incredible opportunity from the Department of Fine Arts at Howard University.

TRUST THE PROCESS

Fortunately, I knew I was interested in Acting when I came to Howard. But, if I had not been open to Professor M changing my major to Musical Theatre, I don't think I would've had this opportunity to travel abroad with such a great cast. I am glad I trusted my professor and took the risk during my freshman year. It gave me the courage to take even more risks later on in life and I began to learn to simply enjoy the ride. I encourage you to trust the process of your life as it unfolds. There are so many magical experiences waiting to reveal themselves to you.

EXPLORE NEW CULTURE

The Chinese' hospitality and way of life was so refreshing. I enjoyed learning briefly about their cultural traditions and etiquette practices. Many of the people were very polite and patient with us as we tried to understand their English translations and they tried to understand our attempts at speaking in their Mandarin language. The honest and sincere exchanges showed great respect for both of our countries. In those moments, I thought maybe the world was not as unfamiliar as I had expected. There are many ways to communicate and express oneself, but the desire and opportunity to learn from one another appears to be mutual. As you consider studying abroad, research the location of your choice and be prepared to make life long memories that will enhance your life and hopefully cause you to appreciate the lifestyles of others around the world.

THE SHOW MUST GO ON

When we were asked to perform prior to the show, the Chinese Ambassadors never knew how sick we were. I think that was due to the training we received at Howard. We never let them see us 'sweat.' Professor M always pushed us passed our limits to reach our greatness and the guest speakers who visited informed us of the discipline required to succeed in our profession. "The show must go on" was heard quite often. In some cases, we were reminded that there would always be someone waiting in the wings ready to take our place. It would be up to us to fight for what was ours at all times. This competitive approach not only made us stronger as professional performers, but it made us stronger as maturing individuals. Life will always throw you curve balls and in some instances, it will be important to recognize what you can and cannot handle. But in most instances, life will test your ability to rise to the occasion and put forth your best effort. Look out for those tests and be prepared to turn them into your testimonies.

THE POWER OF CONNECTION

Meeting some of the audience members after our premier show was one of the highlights of our visit. We were able to connect with people who mutually enjoyed the arts as much as we did, and valued us as individuals with dreams yet to be fulfilled. In that way, we were all the same. I could see the determination in their eyes to succeed in their pursuits and they saw it in ours. I wish I had more time to learn about their individual stories. After many hugs and well wishes, we left one another holding each other accountable for making our dreams come true. If you decide to travel abroad, make it point to learn about someone's personal story and then share yours. You just might discover a connection that could lead to a lifelong friendship!

BE ACCOUNTABLE!

FOOD FOR THOUGHT

Trust the Process
Can you recall a time when you were unsure about an outcome, but you decided to 'trust the process'? If so, how did you feel afterwards?

_____

_____

_____

_____

Study Abroad
Do you plan to study abroad for a semester during your college experience? If so, what do you want to learn about the culture when you get there?

_____

_____

_____

_____

How will you prepare yourself for the visit and manage living in a foreign country for a period of time?

_____

_____

_____

_____

How do you plan to make genuine connections with people from a foreign land?

_____

_____

_____

_____

The **Back to Me** Devotional

Chapter 9

HEADLIGHTS

"You gain strength, courage and confidence by every experience in which you really stop to look fear in the face...You must do the thing you think you can not do." **Eleanor Roosevelt**

"Now I'm approaching my destiny. This time I'll be ready!"
Headlights Lyric
from my 'Back to Me' Album

"So then, each of us will give an account of ourselves to God."
Romans 14:12 NIV

WHEN FAME GETS UNCOMFORTABLE

Returning back to the US as an international performer filled me with an even greater determination to be a professional in my field for the rest of my life! I had discovered a new level of confidence in my abilities as an artist and as a human being. Until...

The Miss Fine Arts Pageant was coming up and many of my friends, along with Professor M suggested I give it a shot. I never thought about competing in a beauty

pageant and I definitely didn't want to parade around
the stage in a bikini for the whole school. But, I was quickly
corrected and told there would be no need for bikinis.
However, I needed to craft a performance and an essay
explaining why I would be the best person to represent
our school in the Miss Howard Pageant. I though to myself,
"The Miss Howard Pageant? I may not even make the cut
for Miss Fine Arts and they're talking about Miss Howard
already? How did I get myself into this?" Professor M
believed in me when he met me in my freshman year and
he hadn't steered me wrong yet. So, I decided to give it
try. After all, it would give me an opportunity to start
performing as a solo artist for my school!

I was certainly nervous about the idea of making it all the
way to the Miss Howard Pageant because I was used
to performing for my peers in my department, but to
possibly get the chance to perform alone for the entire
university was a totally different thing. I wanted to be sure
I could do it and represent our school and myself well.

A few weeks later, Professor M called me to his office
to tell me the team of judges reviewed my essay
and believed my performances from previous shows
demonstrated my ability to best represent the school
in the Miss Howard Pageant as Miss Fine Arts! I said,
"Come again?" I couldn't believe I was selected! What?
Me? Were they sure? Professor M assured me that I
was selected and it was time for me to prepare my best
solo performance for the talent portion of the pageant.
After repeatedly asking Professor M if he was sure, he
reminded me that I could do anything I put my mind to.
If I wanted to give the opportunity to someone else by
declining the offer, I certainly had that option. I slowly
picked up my bottom jaw and immediately told him, "No,

I can do it. Thank you for selecting me. Please thank the other judges as well. I will give it my all and make you all proud!"

With that I was off and running. Crafting my best solo performance for the pageant became my only focus. I decided to perform "A Song for You' by Donny Hathaway.

 THAT SONG WAS THE PERFECT LOVE LETTER TO EVERY AUDIENCE MEMBER AND EVERY PERSON WHO HAD EVER ENCOURAGED ME TO BE AN ENTERTAINER.

I thought about the first time I ever sang for my mother's church, the few times in high school I sang and performed an interpretive dance for my recitals, the time 'Amazing Grace' inspired Professor M to change my major, and the heartfelt applause from the audiences in night clubs and in theatres here and all the way in Hong Kong. I wanted this performance to pay homage to all of those unforgettable moments of connection. Because of them, music became my life and they all played a magical part in helping me discover my voice.

The night of the pageant had arrived and the highly anticipated talent portion of the competition began. "I've been so many places in my life and time. I've sung a lot of songs. I made some bad rhymes. I've acted out my life in stages with 10,000 people watching. But we're alone now and I'm singing this song to you." For my performance, I belted out those words from Donny Hathaway's powerful song and the audience erupted. My stage was set up like a dressing room. I had entered with exhaustion as if I had just completed a concert. The lights dimmed and I was alone with my thoughts and my audience. I took off my sequined jacket and headed to the front of the stage and sang my heart out to the huge Howard audience in front of me. My performance was my love letter to them. As the audience quietly listened, I could feel our connection. They were drawn in and I was drawn in to them. The solo performance that I worried so much about was paying off. I was living out my dreams through this song. All I'd ever been taught and all I'd ever known to do was inspire people through music. It was happening on a bigger stage and the jitters I felt initially were no longer there. I was alone with my audience and I was singing that song to them.

After my performance, I realized I had a tear-stained face, but they were tears of joy. I was happy I made it through the song. But, I was even happier the audience applauded and cheered out loud! This was yet another risk I had taken and I came out stronger on the other side. I no longer worried about living up to the image of what I thought Miss Fine Arts was supposed to be or even what some people had expected this former Dreamgirl to be. I was finally at peace with myself and my relationship with the stage. I knew I had already won before the winner was announced. I came to Howard to find Ms. Debbie Allen's 'fame', and instead I found me. I found my calling.

I didn't win the pageant. I placed 4th in the competition. I think it was because I flubbed my interview question. I was asked, "If you could be any stage performer in the world, who would it be and why?" I wanted to say, "Me!"

But, I hesitated a while and thought my response would not be received well since I was only just discovering who I was. I didn't want to come across as some sort of self-righteous performer who was too full of herself. So, I finally said, "Uh, uh, I think, uh, I think Josephine Baker because of her appeal to people around the world as an artist and a philanthropist. She changed children's lives and I hope to be like her someday."

An Engineering student was actually crowned that year as Miss Howard. She deserved it and I was very happy for her. But, I couldn't help feeling like I had accomplished something incredible that night too. I would have loved to win the crown, but my baby steps toward self-discovery were becoming greater leaps toward to a better understanding of myself and I was proud of that.

MAKE AN IMPACT WITH YOUR CRAFT
Being selected to represent my department was certainly more than an honor, it was a privilege. Although I was scared out of my mind, I was grateful for the acknowledgement. Professor M, along with my other amazing professors believed in my abilities and nurtured me throughout my college experience. They taught me to believe in myself and to use my craft to impact the lives of others. Once you identify your true passion for your college major, make sure it will ultimately serve you and the people around you.

FIND YOUR STRENGTH ON THE OTHER SIDE
Your journey will be full of ups and downs, but the bumpy ride will be worth it. As you make your way through every experience, embrace your fear. Use fear to motivate you to stretch and grow. If you think you can't do something, try it anyway. Expand your perception of yourself. You are capable of more than you think. But, you'll only find

out if you keep moving forward to see what's around the corner. Prepare as best you can and proceed with caution, but keep moving forward. Pageantry was never something I imagined doing, but it actually served a greater purpose. It helped me push past who I thought I should be, only to discover who I truly wanted to be. Fear did that and it can do the same for you. Take a deep breath and enjoy the ride!

BE AUTHENTICALLY YOU

I'll never know if I would've won the pageant had I been more polished or more prepared to answer that interview question. But, I know that I did my best in that moment. Doubting one's self is a part of the journey. You won't really know how to overcome it until you experience it. When I think about that moment and the resistance I felt to give my initial and authentic response, I felt slightly defeated inside. I wanted to say, "Me!" but instead I chose the safe route and gave a safe response to a powerful question. I don't beat myself up about it anymore because I realize why I responded the way I did. I made the assumption of what I thought others would think of me instead of being true to how I felt in the moment. This will happen to you in this life and you too may choose to take the safe route. But, I challenge you to acknowledge your self-doubt when it rears its ugly head, and respond authentically!

GET READY!
YOUR DESTINY IS APPROACHING!

FOOD FOR THOUGHT

Community Impact
How will your college major serve you and impact the lives of others?

_____

_____

_____

_____

If you're still unsure of your major, have you scheduled your next appointment with your counselor or professor to get more clarity around your choice?

_____

_____

Self Doubt
Have you ever taken the safer route in life because of your own self-doubt? If so, why do you think you hesitated?

_____

_____

_____

_____

What action steps do you take to defeat self-doubt and maintain your authenticity?

_____

_____

The **Back to Me** Devotional

SURRENDER

"When I let go of what I am, I become what I might be." **Lao Tzu**

"I wanna live. I'm gonna fly. All of my days, You've never denied.
So, I surrender to Your love forever!"
Surrender Lyric from my 'Back to Me' Album

"For whoever wants to save their life will lose it, but whoever loses
their life for Me and for the gospel will save it." **Mark 8:35 NIV**

HAPPINESS IS A CHOICE

My four-year college experience taught me many things
about myself and the goals I planned to accomplish
outside of that safe and nurturing environment. I will
never forget the constant laughter of my peers in the
halls of the Fine Arts building. Together, we grew leaps
and bounds through our workshops, auditions, and
travels abroad. I will forever be connected to them and
those unforgettable moments. They were there for me
in my greatest moments and during my darkest days.

 The **Back to Me** Devotional

Yes, I was attacked during my senior year. But in the aftermath, I was protected all along. My God never left me. He surrounded me with loving people who made sure I stayed focused on the real prize, my destiny!

After many fond memories and bittersweet goodbyes before graduation, Professor M met with all of us individually for our exit interviews. I remember being so excited to hug and thank him for all he had done for me. He became more than the professor I sought out my freshman year, he was my father in the arts. He saw things in me I never did and he pushed me harder than anyone ever had. He believed in me and that made it easier for me to believe in myself. Even though I was leaving Howard, I knew I had a lifelong mentor in Professor M. I also knew I would always keep in touch with him to share the adventures of my next chapter.

As I waited once again in the hallways to be called in for my final interview, a familiar feeling of anticipation flooded my body. Four years ago, I traveled across the country from California to Washington, DC to meet a professor who would change my life. He ended up doing more than that. He transformed the way I saw myself in the world and for that I am eternally grateful. This time, I was sitting in that same hallway yet again waiting my turn. When I was finally called, I walked onto the stage for the last time to hear the parting words from my dear Professor M. I couldn't help but feel an overwhelming sense of sadness for leaving this magical place and excitement for what was to come in my life. I cautiously sat in the chair that was set center stage and thought about what I hoped he would say to me. He sat in the front row of the auditorium with a very different demeanor than the one he had on the day we met. He appeared to be slightly sad, but proud at the same time. The moment he began to speak, everything became a blur. As I attempted to listen to his words, the flashbacks of my time there all came flooding back and overshadowed anything he was saying. I knew he was giving me some pretty powerful advice, but I was so consumed in my thoughts and my feelings of missing this whole experience that I didn't even hear what he said to me. I just remember getting emotional and trying my best to keep it together while he spoke. At the end of my interview, I assured him I would keep in touch. He wasn't much of a hugger, but I believe we embraced and I walked out just before I began to cry.

As luck would have it, Gary, one of my dear friends was in the auditorium during my interview. He remembered everything Professor M told me. Later, I learned Professor M talked about how much he thought I had grown over the past four years. He encouraged me to stay the course and use everything I experienced there and everything I would experience in the future for my craft. I was told to use the good and the bad in every situation, so I could put it into my art. Wow! What an amazing gift of wisdom! I was very lucky to have a friend in the room who experienced my final interview with me.

 I THINK GOD KNEW THOSE FINAL DAYS WOULD BE VERY EMOTIONAL FOR ME AND HE PLANTED MY FRIEND, GARY THERE JUST IN CASE.

Although, I was an emotional wreck, I left that auditorium feeling like the sky was the limit! I was ready to let my art lead me to my next destination. Professor M used to tell me my talent would take me anywhere I wanted to go if I

allowed it to happen. It was up to me to nurture my gifts and simply embrace what was to come.

STAY FOCUSED
It is understandable and very easy to start worrying about what you will do after college. You just spent four years in an environment you became very comfortable with only to step out into the world yet again. When your time comes, remind yourself of how excited you were to come to college in the first place. The adventures you looked forward to will continue in the next chapter of your life. So, take the time to celebrate the accomplishment of your college experience. Congratulate yourself for completing the task and commit to the goals you set for yourself and your life while you were there.

NURTURE GENUINE RELATIONSHIPS
The great advantage of attending college is the access and the exposure you get to so many different people on one campus. Students come from all of over the world and you have the unique opportunity to make lasting relationships with people whose dreams are just as big as yours. Take the time to make lasting relationships with people during these years. You will be grateful you did. Having their support and knowing they are routing for you as you move forward in life will help motivate you to stay the course and focus on being your best self.

USE THE GOOD AND THE BAD
Don't worry about the naysayers. They will serve a purpose. They are there to remind you of your greatness. Many of them will only appear when they realize you are headed for greener pastures and they are not invited. Don't be surprised if some of these naysayers turn out to be hometown friends, who became slightly envious of your new pursuits or even family members, who found it

hard to celebrate your accomplishments with you. Many of them will mean well, but your success will serve as a reminder of what they too could have accomplished if they had given themselves a fighting chance. The loss of friendship and the change in relationships will cause you pain, but use it to push you one step closer to the purpose for your life. Be compassionate to others, but choose to define yourself for yourself. Like a 'diamond in the rough', you are in the refining process. When you ultimately shine bright, make everything you went through count.

EMBRACE THE UNKNOWN

Every door that will open from this point forward will come with its own set of pleasant surprises and unwanted challenges. Use your meditative practices, keep your supportive relationships close, and remain thankful for every opportunity to learn more about yourself in every circumstance. Try not to anticipate what is around every corner. Instead, embrace the unknown and open yourself up to new and interesting people, places, and things. They will all propel you to your next level. When you get really good at allowing life to happen instead of running away from it, your happiness will be waiting for you on the other side.

GO GET YOUR HAPPINESS!

FOOD FOR THOUGHT

College and Beyond

What do you hope to accomplish after you graduate from college, both personally and professionally?

_____

_____

What qualities will you require in the relationships you make going forward?

_____

_____

How will you handle the naysayers that come into your life as you climb your personal ladder to success? What will you do to stay motivated?

_____

_____

_____

_____

How would you define 'happiness' in your life? Do you have it now? If not, how do you plan to achieve it?

_____

_____

_____

_____

_____

_____

ABOUT THE AUTHOR

YOLI TAMU (also known as Yolonda Tamu Snell) enjoys performing and offering her insights to help empower women of all ages. She is an educator and singer/ songwriter who believes in the positive reinforcement and personal development of young women. As the founder of the Unity Theatre Foundation, a 501(c)3 nonprofit organization designed to serve as an outlet of creative expression for young people, Yoli credits the performing arts education she received for helping build her self-confidence, enhance her social development, and spark her desire to inspire others to fulfill their dreams. For the past 18 years, Yoli has taught elementary, high school and college students. She understands the challenges young people face growing up in this ever-changing world. She earned a Master of Education Degree in Cross-Cultural Teaching from National University in La Jolla, California, and a Bachelor of Fine Arts Degree in Musical Theatre from Howard University in Washington, D.C.

Yoli is also a former Warner Bros. Records label recording artist who has co-written songs for film and television. One of her notable theme songs, "Ain't No Stoppin' Sunshine," can be heard in the cherished and acclaimed motion picture, "Deliver Us from Eva," starring Gabrielle Union and LL Cool J. This is her first book and she is excited to give her readers an inside look behind the music and her journey into womanhood.